YOUR SECRET SELF

YOUR SECRET SELF

*Understand Yourself and Others Using
the Myers-Briggs Personality Test*

Barbara G. Cox, Ed.S.

WINDHORSE
B O O K S

WINDHORSE BOOKS
Gainesville, Florida
www.WindhorseBooks.com

About the Author

Barbara Cox, Ed.S., holds a graduate degree in mental health counseling with a major in personality theory. She has administered the Myers-Briggs test to clients and interpreted the results for over twenty years. Her Internet blog gets over 200,000 visitors per month.

Acknowledgment

Without the support of Sharon Julien, talented artist and website designer, this book would have been nothing more than a fantasy. Sharon designed the cover, made important content suggestions, and helped take it through the complex process of publication. Carolina Madera contributed her outstanding organizational skills to the final production of the book. Stephanie Anderson, Jera Publishing, lent her design expertise to the interior.

Windhorse Books
5429 SW 80 Street
Gainesville, FL 32608

ISBN 978-0-9973745-2-0

Printed in the United States of America

Contents

Chapter 1

Psychological Tests and the Secrets They Reveal

*T*he Myers-Briggs Type Inventory is one of many psychological tests developed in the U.S. since the early 1900s. You've probably taken several over the years—tests measuring your intelligence, emotional balance, motivation, and so on. There's almost nothing about your mind that psychological tests can't measure—from intelligence to character. In the last few decades, personality inventories have become popular with educators and employers as a way to evaluate people's work styles and ability to get along with others.

Most Popular Psychological Tests

Some of the most widely used psychological tests are the Stanford-Binet Intelligence Test, Minnesota Multiphasic

Personality Inventory (MMPI), Thematic Apperception Test (TAT), Rorschach Inkblot Test, Enneagram, and Myers–Briggs Type Indicator. The Myers-Briggs Type Indicator is the most popular.

Stanford-Binet Intelligence Test

Intelligence tests first appeared in France in 1912, created by a Paris psychologist. The Binet test was imported to the United States, translated into English, and refined at Stanford University in 1916. As the test developed over the years, a score of 100 was taken to be average for any given age. People scoring below 90 were thought to be delayed cognitively. Those with scores above 145 were considered gifted.

Minnesota Multiphasic Personality Inventory (MMPI)

The Minnesota Multiphasic Personality Inventory (MMPI) is used to evaluate mental health problems. With over 500 questions, the test identifies symptoms of depression, anxiety, passivity, and even addiction potential. Topics covered by the inventory include religion, politics, sex, health, family life, education, work, and other social issues. Not only do responses show facets of the test-taker's personality, they reveal inconsistent or deceptive answers. The MMPI is a useful diagnostic tool, as well as a guide to treatment.

Thematic Apperception Test (TAT)

The Thematic Apperception Test (TAT) was developed as a projective psychological test. Subjects are given a series of unlabeled drawings and asked to make up a story about each. The pictures are ambiguous in meaning. The stories reveal the test-takers' motivations, concerns, and ways of looking at the social world. Since its introduction in the mid-1900s, the TAT has been widely used to evaluate attitudes and emotions in people from the ages of seven and up.

Rorschach Inkblot Test

The Rorschach Inkblot Test is another projective tool. It consists of mirror images of complex inkblots that can suggest any number of themes. Test-takers are asked to tell the psychologist what they see in the various images. The results are believed to reveal subjects' underlying beliefs and emotions.

Enneagram

The Enneagram is an inventory of questions about people's perceptions of themselves. The system categorizes test-takers in nine basic personality types, each identified by a number and a name. For example, Types 1, 2, and 3 are identified as the Reformer, the Helper, and the Achiever, respectively. While the Enneagram is rarely used for psychological research, it is widely used in business management and as a self-help tool.

Myers-Briggs Type Indicator

The Myers-Briggs test evaluates personality according to how people perceive their world, make decisions, and interact with others. It's based on the theories of Carl Jung, Swiss psychoanalyst. In the 1940s, Katharine Cook Briggs and her daughter Isabel Briggs Myers developed a system of Jungian personality types that could be categorized by a self-administered inventory. According to the theory, people have preferences in the way they construe their experiences, and these help determine their personality type.

Chapter 2

How the Myers-Briggs
Test Works

*I*sabel Myers and her mother, Katharine Briggs—
both psychologists— developed the Myers-Briggs
Personality Inventory more than fifty years ago. They
were looking for a way to classify different types of personalities and describe them using the theories of Carl
Jung, the famous Swiss psychoanalyst.

Myers and Briggs wanted to create a test people
could take to help them understand themselves and others. Their personality inventory was first published in
1975. Its practical applications have been expanding ever
since—in schools and colleges, businesses, counselors'
offices, and other settings.

The test is based on the idea that there are four
pairs of personality traits that influence how we think,
feel and act. Each pair represents a continuum. The

far ends of each continuum are like opposite sides of a coin. The preference pairs can be thought of in relation to their function. The first pair—introversion (I) and extraversion (E)—involve the use and conservation of energy. The second pair—sensing (S) and intuition (N)—determine where a person's attention is focused. The third pair—thinking (T) and feeling (F)— form the basis of decision-making. The fourth pair—perceiving (P) and judging (J)—are attitude preferences, determining whether the person takes an open-ended approach to life or prefers closure in most situations.

While some people are at the extreme end of a trait continuum, most are somewhere in between. However, even those who score at one end or the other are capable of thinking and behaving like their opposites some of the time. Meyers and Briggs believed that the traits by which a person is classified are more a matter of preference than "hard wiring."

Energy Preferences

Introversion (I)
Introverts gather their energy from thinking and reflecting in private. Exposure to groups of people for long periods drains them. Extraverts draw energy from the

company of others. They need the stimulation of people and social activities.

If you're an introvert, you probably need lots of private time—periods when you won't be interrupted by others. You focus inwardly on your thoughts and tasks, seldom talk about them, and get irritated if people distract you. You come across as reserved to many people.

You're suspicious of people who seem too glib. You think, "Talk is cheap," and wish people would do less of it. If you need to spend time in a group for social or business reasons, you're glad when you can leave and relax. You'd prefer to be at home alone or spending time with one other person in a quiet setting.

Extraversion (E)

Extraverts usually know a lot of people and consider many of them friends. If you're an extravert, you don't mind being where a lot is going on at once. You aren't distracted by the TV, radio, or conversations of others. While people find you friendly and easy to approach, they may feel that you tend to dominate conversations. At parties, you mix easily with other guests, approaching strangers as readily as friends. Because talking is perfectly natural to you, you may reveal more about yourself than you realize without learning a great deal about others. To feel sure of yourself, you probably need frequent attention and affirmation.

Attention Preferences

Sensing (S)

Sensing types focus on what they see, hear, and feel in front of them. They rely more on their five senses than on intellectual functions or imagination. Intuitive types require less external information to stimulate their thought processes. They're attentive to underlying meaning and potential for the future.

If you prefer sensing to intuition, you'd rather work with facts and figures than ideas or theories. You want to be given clear directions and prefer concrete tasks with measurable outcomes. When assembling something, you follow the printed instructions. You're orderly in your approach to work and leisure activities. You aren't as concerned with how events fit into the larger scheme of things as you are about their immediate meaning.

Intuition (N)

If you're an intuitive type, you rely on your intuition to find the connections between things. The future and its possibilities are more attractive than the present. You seldom take people and events at face value.

You find details boring and follow directions only when necessary. You'd rather figure things out for yourself. You get annoyed with people who are always literal and direct and who lack subtle wit. You're more interested in why things are happening than what's actually happening.

Decision Preferences

Thinking (T)

Thinkers prefer to collect information in a logical way, organize it, and then base their decisions on hard data. They try to leave emotions out of the decision-making process. While feeling types also collect and organize information, they create a structure for decision-making that's based on personal values. They are concerned about the outcome of their decisions on others.

If you're a thinker, you're firm and direct and don't sugarcoat your opinions. You pride yourself on your ability to be rational. While some people may accuse you of being too objective, you consider yourself fair. You usually stay calm and collected when others are upset. You think it's more important to be right in your judgments than have others like you. You prefer information that's scientific and logical rather than anecdotal.

Feeling (F)

If you're a feeling type, you prefer harmony above all else. Confrontation is difficult for you and you try to avoid or camouflage it. If you offend someone, you're quick to back off and apologize. Sometimes people consider you wishy-washy. You enjoy helping others. In fact, you're inclined to overextend yourself at the expense of your own comfort.

Attitude Preferences

Perceiving (P)

Perceiving types look around them and respond to people and events in a more spontaneous way than judging types. They are flexible in their attitudes and habits and tend to be more easy-going. Judgers prefer planning and organization, disliking unexpected surprises.

If you're a perceiver, you welcome new ways of doing things. When you have a task to do, you seldom plan ahead. You prefer to see what's needed as you go along. Your tendency to improvise and ignore time limitations sometimes makes you late for appointments and meeting deadlines. This can frustrate colleagues and family, who may accuse you of being disorganized. You have the gift of turning work into play, figuring that if it isn't fun, it probably isn't worth doing. While you would prefer an orderly environment, creativity and spontaneity are more important.

Judging (J)

If you are a judging type, you're rarely late for anything, whether it be an appointment or a work deadline. You follow schedules and make lists. Days that get chaotic and don't go as planned frustrate you. You tend to have fixed opinions and expectations of others. Sometimes people think you're angry when you're only stating your opinion. You don't appreciate surprises, even pleasant ones. You like to be prepared for all eventualities.

Sixteen Types Overview

When the preferences are grouped in all possible combinations of personality types, there are sixteen, as shown below. Each type is named by the four letters that stand for the preferences that predominate for a person. I = introvert, E = extravert, S = sensing, N = intuitive, T = thinking, F = feeling, P = perceiving, and J = judging.

ENFJ—*Most persuasive*
Charismatic, idealistic,
avoids conflict.
Compassionate, sees
others' potential.

ENFP—*Most optimistic*
Outgoing, creative.
Better at starting than
finishing things.

ENTJ—
Most commanding
Outgoing, argumentative,
impatient with
incompetence.
Good at planning,
implementing ideas.

ENTP—*Most inventive*
Enthusiastic, innovative.
Likes to debate about
ideas, take risks.

ESFJ—*Most harmonious*
Courteous, thoughtful,
eager to please. Has good
interpersonal skills, is a
model host or hostess.

ESFP—*Most generous*
Outgoing, loves
surprises, generous, gets
to the heart of matters.
Juggles projects easily.

ESTJ—*Most forceful*
Results-oriented, orderly,
traditional. Outgoing and
sociable, but opinionated.

ESTP—
Most entertaining
Fun to be with, outgoing,
lives in the now.
Good problem-solver,
unconventional.

INFJ—*Most reflective*
Introspective, quietly
caring, creative.
Articulate and visionary.

INFP—*Most idealistic*
Creative, nondirective,
reserved. Holds strong
personal values,
seeks harmony.

INTJ—*Most independent*
Skeptical, values
competence,
often impatient.
Perfectionistic,
independent.

INTP—*Most conceptual*
Absent-minded,
reflective, independent.
Often competitive,
challenging others.

ISFJ—*Most loyal*
Easy to work with,
generous, dependable.
Sacrifices readily to
help others.

ISFP—*Most artistic*
Warm, gentle, sensitive.
Cooperates well with
others, in touch with self
and nature.

ISTJ—*Most dependable*
Private, organized,
reliable, practical.
Follows rules.

ISTP—*Most observant*
Sees everything,
says little. Practical,
unpretentious, ready
for anything.

The types are described
more fully in the chapters
that follow the test.

Chapter 3

Take the Personality Test

*T*he test in this chapter will identify which of the 16 Myers-Briggs types most applies to you. When you read the questions, choose the best answer. If neither answer seems quite right, pick the one that's better than the other.

A scoring key appears at the end of the test.

1. At a party, which do you do?
   a) Talk with many people, including strangers.
   b) Talk with a few people you know.

2. In what terms do you like to think best?
   a) What "is."
   b) What "might be."

3. Which is worse?
   a) To have your head in the clouds.
   b) To be in a rut.

4. Which do you go by more?

   a) Rules and principles.

   b) Feelings and emotions.

5. What influences you more?

   a) A story backed up by convincing facts.

   b) A story that's touching.

6. How do you like to work best?

   a) Under deadlines.

   b) "Whenever."

7. How do you make up your mind?

   a) Rather carefully.

   b) Somewhat impulsively.

8. At parties, which are you more likely to do?

   a) Stay late, getting more energized as the evening goes on.

   b) Leave early, running out of energy as the evening goes on.

9. Which kind of people do you like best?

   a) Sensible people.

   b) Creative people.

10. Which are you more interested in?
    a) What's in the here and now.
    b) What's possible in the future.

11. When deciding if someone is right or wrong, what are you more swayed by?
    a) Rules and laws applying to that person's case.
    b) Circumstances in that person's case.

12. When you want something from somebody, how do you tend to be?
    a) Matter of fact.
    b) Personal.

13. When you're going someplace, which describes you better?
    a) Always on time.
    b) Casual about time.

14. Which bothers you more?
    a) To leave something unfinished.
    b) To bring something to a finish.

15. In groups you're involved in, which are you more likely to do?
    a) Keep up with what's happening with everybody.
    b) Get behind on the news.

16. How do you usually go about tasks?
    a) The usual way.
    b) My own way.

17. How should writers say things?
    a) In a straightforward way.
    b) By making comparisons or giving examples.

18. Which do you prefer?
    a) Logic and consistency.
    b) Getting along with people.

19. When you have to judge something, how would you prefer to do it?
    a) On a logical basis.
    b) On the basis of values.

20. How do you like things best?
    a) Settled and decided.
    b) Open-ended.

21. Which describes you better?
    a) Serious and determined.
    b) Easy-going.

22. Before phoning someone, what do you do?
    a) Not think about what will be said.
    b) Rehearse what I'll say.

23. What is the main benefit of facts?
    a) To speak for themselves.
    b) To illustrate principles.

24. How do you feel about creative geniuses?
    a) They're somewhat annoying.
    b) They're rather fascinating.

25. Which do you consider yourself more?
    a) A cool-headed person.
    b) A warmhearted person.

26. Which is worse?
    a) To be unjust.
    b) To be without mercy.

27. How do you like to have things happen?
    a) By planning ahead and making careful choices.
    b) By letting things happen by chance.

28. What makes you feel better?
    a) Buying something and taking it home.
    b) Thinking about buying something.

29. When you're with others, what do you do?
    a) Usually start the conversation.
    b) Wait for someone else to start talking.

30. How do you view "common sense"?
    a) It's usually right.
    b) It's often wrong.

31. Which should children do more?
    a) Make themselves useful to others.
    b) Be fanciful and creative.

32. When you make a decision, which helps you the most?
    a) Thinking it through logically.
    b) Going by feelings.

33. Which do you consider yourself?
    a) More firm than gentle.
    b) More gentle than firm.

34. Which do you admire more?
    a) Being able to organize things well.
    b) Being flexible and able to "make do."

35. Which way are you more comfortable?
    a) Being definite.
    b) Being open-ended.

36. When you're with new people for a period of time, how do you feel?
    a) Energized.
    b) Taxed.

37. Which describes you better?
    a) Mostly a practical, sensible person.
    b) More of a dreamer who sees possibilities.

38. How do you tend to view people?
    a) By their usefulness in my life.
    b) As people with their own perspectives.

39. Which do you like better?

    a) To discuss an issue thoroughly.
    b) To reach an agreement about the issue.

40. Which are you ruled by more?

    a) Your head.
    b) Your heart.

41. What kind of work do you prefer?

    a) Work on a contract with a deadline.
    b) Work on a casual basis.

42. How do you like to have things happen in the future?

    a) In an orderly way.
    b) In a random way.

43. Which do you prefer to have?

    a) Many friends, brief contact with each.
    b) Few friends, longer contact with each.

44. How are you more likely to decide things?

    a) By facts.
    b) By principles.

45. If you were offered two jobs, which would you choose?
    a) Producing and distributing widgets.
    b) Designing and doing research on widgets.

46. Which is more of a compliment?
    a) There's a very logical person.
    b) There's a very sentimental person.

47. How would you prefer to be?
    a) Consistent and unwavering.
    b) Devoted and committed.

48. Which kind of statement do you prefer?
    a) Clear statement that won't be changed.
    b) Tentative statement that's open to change.

49. When are you more comfortable?
    a) After a decision has been made.
    b) Before a decision has been reached.

50. When you're with strangers, which are you more likely to do?
    a) Speak easily and at length.
    b) Find little to say.

51. Which do you trust more?
    a) Experience.
    b) Hunches.

52. Which best describes you?
    a) More practical than creative.
    b) More creative than practical.

53. Which is a bigger compliment?
    a) To be a person of clear reason.
    b) To be a person of strong feeling.

54. Which are you more inclined to be?
    a) Fair-minded.
    b) Sympathetic.

55. Which do you think is better?
    a) To make sure things are arranged.
    b) To just let things happen.

56. In relationships which is better?
    a) To negotiate things as you go along.
    b) To let things happen in a random way,
        according to circumstances.

57. When the phone rings, what do you do?
    a) Hurry to get it first.
    b) Hope someone else will answer it.

58. Which do you value more in yourself?
    a) A strong sense of reality.
    b) A vivid imagination.

59. When you read something, what are you more influenced by?
    a) Basic facts.
    b) Overtones.

60. Which is worse?
    a) To be too passionate.
    b) To be too cool-headed.

61. Which describes you better?
    a) Hard-headed.
    b) Soft-hearted.

62. How do you like things better?
    a) Planned ahead, scheduled.
    b) Not planned ahead, not scheduled.

63. Which describes you better?

    a) More routine than creative.

    b) More creative than routine.

64. What kind of writing do you prefer?

    a) Direct and literal.

    b) Indirect and figurative.

65. Which would you prefer to have?

    a) Reason and clear thinking.

    b) Feeling and compassion.

66. Which do you like better?

    a) An event that's planned ahead.

    b) An event that's unplanned and spontaneous.

Scoring Key

Put a check for each answer in the a column or the b column. Then mark the totals at the bottom of each column.

1. a __ b __	2. a __ b __	4. a __ b __	6. a __ b __
	3. a __ b __	5. a __ b __	7. a __ b __
8. a __ b __	9. a __ b __	11. a __ b __	13. a __ b __
	10. a __ b __	12. a __ b __	14. a __ b __
15. a __ b __	16. a __ b __	18. a __ b __	20. a __ b __
	17. a __ b __	19. a __ b __	21. a __ b __
22. a __ b __	23. a __ b __	25. a __ b __	27. a __ b __
	24. a __ b __	26. a __ b __	28. a __ b __
29. a __ b __	30. a __ b __	32. a __ b __	34. a __ b __
	31. a __ b __	33. a __ b __	35. a __ b __
36. a __ b __	37. a __ b __	39. a __ b __	41. a __ b __
	38. a __ b __	40. a __ b __	42. a __ b __
43. a __ b __	44. a __ b __	46. a __ b __	48. a __ b __
	45. a __ b __	47. a __ b __	49. a __ b __
50. a __ b __	51. a __ b __	53. a __ b __	55. a __ b __
	52. a __ b __	54. a __ b __	56. a __ b __
57. a __ b __	58. a __ b __	60. a __ b __	62. a __ b __
	59. a __ b __	61. a __ b __	63. a __ b __
	64. a __ b __	65. a __ b __	66. a __ b __

Totals

a __ b __	a __ b __	a __ b __	a __ b __
E I	**S N**	**T F**	**J P**

E = Extravert   I = Introvert   S = Sensing   N = Intuitive
T = Thinking   F = Feeling   J = Judging   P = Perceiving

Chapter 4

ENFJ—The Mentor

Extraverted, Intuitive, Feeling, and Judging

Loyal	*Responsible*
Idealistic	*Enthusiastic*
Articulate	*Congenial*
Tactful	*Outgoing*

*E*NFJs are energetic and outgoing. They have a sixth sense for other people's needs and get pleasure from helping them. Their interpersonal skills make others want to join them to make things happen. ENFJs are quick to show their appreciation to friends and co-workers and they're generally well liked.

Being natural extraverts, ENFJs enjoy projects that require teamwork, especially service work. Because they're so enthusiastic and verbal, they're often pushed into leadership positions both at work and in the community. They're effective public speakers and enjoy the limelight. When they take the podium, they're inclined to be verbose if they haven't disciplined themselves to speak concisely.

These natural-born leaders have strong personalities, radiate authenticity, and aren't afraid to stand up and speak their truth. Communicating with others comes easily to them, especially in person. They have an eloquence that helps bring people together in a common cause.

Falling in Love

When ENFJs fall in love, it's all they can think about. They bring gifts to the new partner, write poetry, and arrange candlelit dinners. They like to talk about the relationship a lot, exploring all its aspects and possibilities.

ENFJs tend to think that the honeymoon phase will last forever. The normal ups and downs of a relationship are hard for them to acknowledge and accept. They may sweep problems under the rug that should be dealt with openly. They need to learn that conflict can clear the air and give the parties new information about each other that enables them to interact on a deeper level in the future.

ENFJs don't want to hear anything negative about their partner from friends nor be warned that they've made a bad choice. If a partner cheats on them or breaks up the relationship, they are devastated. They tend to see the failure as a reflection of their own inadequacy. They're ashamed that things didn't work out and feel a sense of blame.

At Work

ENFJs prefer a work environment that's organized and settled, but they don't want it so orderly that there's no room for creativity and problem-solving. They delegate responsibility to others wisely and easily. ENFJs are encouraging with co-workers and subordinates while remaining focused on the goals and ideals of their organization. They like to see their colleagues grow professionally.

ENFJs do best in an atmosphere of cooperation and harmony. They like to coach teams of colleagues. Employees will be expected to abide by the plans developed by the ENFJ and meet deadlines, but exceptions are made when they have personal issues or problems. Then the ENFJ is gracious and accommodating.

On the job, ENFJs may run into trouble when they put socializing before work-related tasks. They tend to take so much pleasure in the company of others that they spend more time discussing personal matters than transacting business.

Home Life

Family comes first with ENFJs. If ENFJs have work they've brought home or personal chores that need doing, these are always put on hold to meet the needs of their partners and children. As a result, it's easy for family members to impose on them. ENFJs have to be careful about letting others take advantage of their easy-going nature.

Most ENFJs spend a good deal of their leisure time reading. They encourage their children to enjoy books, too, taking them to the library frequently and reading to them at bedtime. They like attending movies and plays together. Afterwards, they talk about the plot and characters. It pleases them to encourage their children to observe the world intelligently.

If family members aren't getting along or the ENFJ is having problems with a partner, these matters are likely to be pushed aside as long as possible because ENFJs are averse to conflict. When the happiness and comfort of others is in jeopardy, however, they will intervene to discuss issues in a friendly, creative way. They are good at fostering a cooperative, amiable home environment.

Growing Older

During retirement, ENFJs usually settle near family members or in a community where they have strong personal ties. Relationships continue to take top priority in their lives.

They are hard workers during their years of employment, and they continue to work hard after retirement. The only difference is that they aren't paid for their volunteer work. Meeting others' needs makes them feel alive and worthwhile. Even when they're old and no longer robust, ENFJs push themselves to help people in need.

In addition to community volunteer work, much of their time is used to assist friends and family. If a grandchild needs a ride to a school event, the ENFJ is the first to volunteer. As grandparents, ENFJs frequently overextend themselves, and the grandchildren are quick to take advantage of it.

Chapter 5

ENFP—The Campaigner

Extraverted, Intuitive, Feeling and Perceiving

Enthusiastic	*Creative*
Spontaneous	*Independent*
Insightful	*Versatile*
Articulate	*Congenial*

*E*NFPs are gracious and tolerant of others. They don't like "putting people in boxes." Sometimes their ability to identify with the thoughts and feelings of those around them is almost uncanny. However, when they go too far with their enthusiasm and openness, they may feel confused and adrift until they get grounded again. On these infrequent occasions, they experience restlessness and even irritability that makes them wonder what they're doing and where they're going.

ENFPs are always open to new experiences and challenges. For this reason, they get special pleasure from traveling. It gives them the opportunity to meet interesting people and experience unfamiliar cultures.

Falling in Love

Because ENFPs need approval and affection so much, they may become seductive with prospective partners in an effort to affirm their desirability. This can result in premature sexual intimacy before a sound groundwork is established for a relationship—with a price to be paid later.

ENFPs tend to fall in love a lot. In a new relationship, they're eager to explore all aspects of the partner's personality and try out things they can do together. They shower the person with affection, as they also tend to do with friends and family. The partners of ENFPs generally feel loved unconditionally, but the feeling may lessen if the ENFP finds some new infatuation—even if it's only a passing fancy.

As long as relationships last, ENFPs are grateful for the best aspects of their partners' personalities. They idealize them and ignore traits that one day might prove to be inconvenient or annoying. When they find flaws that they can no longer overlook, they're pained by the idea of having invested so much of themselves in an arrangement that appears to be falling apart.

When ENFPs aren't the ones to end a relationship, they're deeply hurt. Feeling scorned, they overemphasize the partner's shortcomings and tell friends they're glad to be out of it. Even though such endings are difficult, ENFPs rebound quickly.

At Work

ENFPs prefer careers that are service-oriented and that benefit others. They like their work settings to be colorful and challenging, where people enjoy collegial relationships. Competitive, hard-driving environments are stressful for ENFPs and hamper their ability to perform. As bosses, they encourage their employees to share their insights and allow them to participate in the decision-making process. They prefer a minimum of rules and schedules.

ENFPs are outgoing, friendly, and energetic. They're able to deal with many situations in the workplace at once without being overwhelmed. They see possibilities all around them and turn them into realities.

ENFPs are good at spotting useful skills and positive qualities in others, which makes them effective delegators. They have amazing insights about group dynamics, why people are behaving in certain ways, and which co-workers are most compatible (or incompatible) with others. The ENFP is often regarded as charismatic by colleagues. They extend themselves to please others, often going overboard in their praise and affirmations. For this reason, sometimes people wonder about their sincerity.

Home Life

ENFPs enjoy parenting, and their children enjoy their family life. ENFPs cope with groups of kids and adults easily and happily. Their home tends to be a neighborhood gathering place. Often they act more like friends than parents, making sure that their kids are allowed to express themselves and reach their full potential. They're not overly concerned with keeping the house orderly or making sure that the rules are followed.

When it's party time, ENFPs are great improvisers and experts at showing people a good time. Spur-of-the moment gatherings are their specialty. They'll come up with everything needed to keep guests entertained. They do have a tendency, afterward, to be self-critical of how well they carried off the event and how they could have done better.

While some Myers-Briggs types have the habit of turning play into work, the opposite is true of ENFPs.

They can make drudgery seem like fun, making sure that everyone has a good time. For family members who are also extraverts, this makes life a pleasure. For those needing more privacy, the ENFP's tendency to turn every occasion into a social event may be annoying and tiring. The children may even consider their parent's behavior immature.

Growing Older

In retirement, many ENFPs enjoy traveling with their families. Visiting new places opens up fresh vistas where together they can learn about different people and cultures. At home, their leisure pursuits usually include sports that let them burn off energy while enjoying the company of others.

Because ENFPs believe in creating a better world for others and happier lives for themselves, they're likely to spend a good deal of retirement time helping people, animals, and the environment.

Chapter 6

ENTJ—The Leader

Extraverted, Intuitive, Thinking and Judging

Logical	*Challenging*
Decisive	*Objective*
Tough	*Fair*
Strategic	*Controlling*

*T*o the ENTJ, the world is a treasure trove of possibilities, all of them within reach. ENTJs are born leaders. Confident and outgoing, they have a need to control the people and circumstances around them. To them, life is full of people who can transform the ENTJ's visions into realities.

ENTJs can be hard on people who fail to live up to their standards. Often their annoyance is out of proportion to whatever has gone wrong. When they lash out impatiently, others can be devastated, even though the

41

storm soon passes and is forgotten by the ENTJ. Some people who find this personality type difficult go out of their way to avoid them. ENTJs are almost always surprised when they learn that they have this effect. They think they're being enthusiastic.

Falling in Love

For ENTJs, falling in love must fit the framework of their lives. A lover takes second place to the ENTJ's life goals, particularly those related to work. In a way, the ENTJ's partner is a supportive actor in the ENTJ's life drama, an extension of his or her personal vision.

ENTJs are demanding partners. They may fall in love readily, but they remain faithful only as long as their partners accept the ENTJ's need for independence and control. ENTJs don't need a lot of emotional support, but when they ask for something, they expect to get it.

Despite their many outside commitments, ENTJs enjoy spending time with their partners and sharing creative, stimulating conversations. Superficial topics bore them. They do best with lovers who are intelligent and share their acute intuition.

Since ENTJs have a high regard for their own positions and are capable of overriding the needs of others, partners must often be the ones to establish limits in a relationship, firmly but tactfully setting boundaries. Most ENTJs have sharp enough intuition to recognize the need for tact if they want to keep a partner.

Because sexual appeal is so important in our culture and ENTJs like to surpass normal standards, they are drawn to attractive partners. It's part of their competitive nature. They want a lover who will complete their own successful image without overshadowing them. Often they look for mates who are more light-hearted and fun-loving, complementing their hard-driving style.

When ENTJs find that their needs are no longer met, they prepare to move on. On the other hand, when the ENTJ is rejected by a lover, he or she may feel a devastating sense of loss. Part of this is due to a reluctance to lose any competition.

At Work

ENTJs prefer an environment that's productive, working among tough-minded colleagues who are smart and independent. Although ENTJs first choice is to lead, they respect those who are more competent. Often, when they're overly impulsive in their decisions, they recognize that input from others is important and listen thoughtfully to advice. Successful ENTJs realize that guidance from quieter, more deliberate types can be a critical factor in their success.

The natural leadership abilities of ENTJs help them rise to the top of their organizations quickly. However, others don't always find them likeable. With their brusque manner and bossy tendencies, they're likely to make enemies along the way. This doesn't bother them much. If they're outvoted by people with better ideas, they demur gracefully and welcome the chance to learn new lessons. Actually, ENTJs appreciate people who stand up to them.

At work, ENTJs take charge of confusing or disorganized situations and turn them around quickly. They define problems and devise strategies to correct them with remarkable clarity. They know how to find the necessary resources to accomplish goals. They're at their best when called upon to use their intuitive powers and analytical ability to overcome challenges.

Home Life

At home, ENTJs are open and honest. They're enthusiastic about activities that their partner and children are involved in and enjoy taking part in them. While outsiders are often afraid of the ENTJ's temper, this is seldom true of family members. They know that the person's bark is worse than his or her bite. However, the family is always aware that the ENTJ is likely to become too managerial if they don't stand up for their rights.

ENTJs enjoy family events. Celebrations give them an excuse to make plans, organize activities, and show off. When the event is under way, they enjoy themselves, laughing and joking with others and participating in whatever activities are involved. They like sitting at the head of the table, presiding over children and relatives.

Growing Older

In retirement, ENTJs don't change much. They still need intellectual activity and excitement. As they adjust to a life free of job responsibilities, they're likely to become less compulsive in their approach to getting things done. They take more time for reflection. Their attempts to control others may decline, especially when family members don't jump to attention the way subordinates once did. ENTJs still like to lead, argue and compete with others, but without the same edge. After a time, they enjoy their more relaxed lifestyle.

Chapter 7

ENTP—The Explorer

Extraverted, Intuitive, Thinking and Perceiving

Enterprising	*Adaptive*
Independent	*Challenging*
Outspoken	*Analytical*
Creative	*Resourceful*

*E*NTPs enjoy a constant flow of inspiration and take pleasure in the company of others. They're always involved in activities that make them and others happy. They jump from one challenge to another, leaving a good many projects unfinished along the way. ENTPs tend to get more excited about thinking up new projects than following through on old ones.

The ability of ENTPs to see the big picture is what motivates their creativity. No matter what the setting—work, home, or leisure—they have ideas about how things can be improved. Often their notions are inspired, as they seem almost clairvoyant about what course the future will take. Because they're so confident of their hunches, they aren't afraid to take risks with resources—their own and those of friends and relatives. When they win, their winnings are big. When they lose, they lose big. Their lives are full of twists and turns.

Falling in Love

ENTPs know pretty quickly when the right person comes along. Often they can tell at the first meeting if the relationship has potential. Until the ideal partner shows up, they are hesitant to commit. They'd rather explore the possibilities of platonic friendship. Because of this, they're not likely to get into serious relationships early in life.

As independent types, ENTPs need freedom to follow their own dreams. Their relationships do best if their partners have high self-esteem and are independent as well.

When a partnership develops, the ENTP may find after a while that it doesn't meet his or her expectations. A partner who was chosen partly on the basis of his or her stability may become boring, causing the ENTP to feel tied down. In such situations, the ENTP usually tries to find a diplomatic way out that will cause minimal distress to the partner. If the partner is responsible for the breakup, ENTPs put their inventive brains to work figuring out why it was destined to fail anyhow. It helps them rationalize their hurt feelings.

Partners who need financial security and an orderly environment may find living with an ENTP chaotic. At some time or another, most ENTP's find themselves on shaky financial footing. An ENTP partnership may not suit the Myers-Briggs type who enjoys a quiet, predictable life.

At Work

ENTPs are creative and enthusiastic, always involved in a variety of projects. Their curious nature is due to their strong intuitive preference, which makes them see life as brimming with possibilities. Because they lean toward theoretical reasoning, they're full of untried ideas. Their ideal workplace is filled with like-minded colleagues solving complex problems. They like careers that focus on change, competency, and risk-taking.

When projects aren't going the way ENTPs think they should, they are clever at persuading co-workers of their point of view and talking them into their solutions. Because they're so persuasive, they can be manipulative and take advantage of other, less quick-thinking folks.

ENTPs resist outmoded bureaucratic structures. They need freedom to act in whatever direction their impulses take them. They're natural entrepreneurs. Jobs based on routines and standard operating procedures frustrate them.

Home Life

The homes of ENTPs are jammed with books, gadgets, and hobby supplies. Children are encouraged to use them all, especially for learning. Neatness and schedules are ignored in the scramble for fun and challenges. Most ENTP parents offer their children more ideas of things to do than they can possibly manage. The kids may miss out on quiet expressions of parental love and relaxing down time with their parents.

ENTPs enjoy family events and are usually the life of the party. They may contribute little to the preparations and turn up late, but they arrive full of energy and ready to turn on the charm. Their behavior is not always appropriate. Sometimes they pick arguments just for the fun of debating. Family members who take no pleasure in competitive exchanges may feel hurt or annoyed.

Growing Older

Retirement is a chance to catch up on long-postponed projects. ENTPs who can pause in their hectic pursuits to reflect and spend time in the quiet company of intimate friends and relatives are likely to calm down and enjoy less hectic lives. Often they find that they're able to indulge in intimate exchanges more than they did in their younger years.

ENTPs enjoy their newfound leisure time, thinking up activities as they go along. The participation of family and friends adds to their pleasure. Travel is particularly inviting as it opens up new vistas and new ways of thinking about their everyday lives.

Chapter 8

ESFJ—The Caretaker

Extraverted, Sensing, Feeling and Judging

Conscientious	*Loyal*
Congenial	*Responsible*
Cooperative	*Tactful*
Compassionate	*Traditional*

*E*SJFs pay attention to the needs of others even when it means putting their own on hold. They're at their best organizing people for family, community or work events. They place a high value on harmony.

As traditionalists, ESFJs rely on tried-and-true methods of solving problems. For this reason, they can overlook newer, better approaches that are obvious to others, a habit that may prove awkward for friends and co-workers who are reluctant to endanger their relationship with the ESFJ by pointing out better methods.

Falling in Love

Love is a totally absorbing experience for ESFJs. They show their affection with gifts, notes, and other symbols of commitment. If the partner admires a new gadget or piece of clothing in a store, the ESFJ will go shopping for it the next day. Even when doing extra favors disrupts their schedule or proves a burden on their pocketbook, ESFJs extend themselves to satisfy the partner's desires, even going to lengths that aren't appropriate or healthy. Some ESFJs may be more in love with love than with their partners per se.

While not demanding, ESFJs do expect some reciprocity. If a lover is not as thoughtful as the ESFJ thinks reasonable, he or she will be disappointed. Still, being practical and realistic, most ESFJs prefer moderation to extravagance.

When partners break up with them, ESFJs are deeply hurt. They need time to recover before showing interest in a new relationship. This is partly due to their tendency to blame themselves. They mentally review the times when they were not as generous or thoughtful as they might have been, even though this assessment may be inaccurate. At worst, ESFJs can develop a deep dislike for the ex-partner. In fact, they may purposely hurt the person with spiteful actions and remarks.

At Work

When possible, ESFJs choose employment where conscientious, value-oriented people like themselves cooperate to help others. They don't fit in well in settings where human values take a back seat to production statistics. At the same time, they need priorities that are clear and relatively unchanging. Their task orientation is based on facts, not abstract concepts.

On the job, ESFJs complete their assignments skillfully and on time. They collaborate well in the workplace. They tackle projects efficiently while respecting the rules and authority of their employers. Although friendly and easy-going in demeanor, they're sharp about business matters. They do whatever they can to ensure a congenial atmosphere and, at the same time, make sure the job gets done.

ESFJs are seldom assertive about seeking leadership roles, but when situations require someone to take charge and no one steps up, the ESFJ will. While earning the goodwill of colleagues, ESFJs set an example of hard work and follow-through. If co-workers fail to meet their standards, the ESFJ seldom berates them openly. Rather, he or she tries to help them make improvements.

Home Life

In their efforts to keep family life harmonious, ESFJs may ignore problems and sweep them under the rug—even when it would be better to let them surface and resolve them with family members. When ESFJs continually fail to value their own priorities and put the needs of others first, they may wear themselves out or become resentful. They need to risk the good will of others by saying "no" when it's justified.

While ESFJs are outgoing and warm at home, they aren't always spontaneous in their use of leisure time. They like things planned in advance. Often they're the ones in charge of traditional get-togethers such as Thanksgiving dinner. They generally take responsibility for buying birthday, anniversary, and holiday gifts.

ESFJs are involved in school and community events. They plan educational or character-building activities for their children, such as after-school sports. Their children may accompany them to Christmas festivities at retirement communities, deliver food to homeless centers, or volunteer at animal shelters. ESFJs give their children valuable lessons in generosity. Most ESFJ parents are highly respected in the community for their warmth, helpfulness, and ability to get things done.

Growing Older

ESFJs continue to be sociable after retirement. They value old friendships and schedule regular activities with the people they've known for years. With their warm personalities, ESFJs may try to sustain work friendships when it's no longer realistic. They don't realize that not all business relationships are meant to be lasting.

When they go too far serving others at home and in the community during retirement, they may overlook their own needs for rest and relaxation in their senior years. They may also make the error of assuming that, as elders, they know what's best for everyone and overstep their bounds. This can make them appear bossy and rigid. Friends can help them manage a graceful retreat in such situations.

Chapter 9

ESFP—The Performer

Extraverted, Sensing, Feeling and Perceiving

Adaptable	*Playful*
Sociable	*Talkative*
Cooperative	*Tolerant*
Easy-going	*Compassionate*

*E*SFPs are outgoing and fun-loving people, drawn to the company of others. Because of their positive attitude, they're usually well liked. They're helpful, too—generous with their time and money. In fact, they'd rather give than receive. They feel self-conscious when praised too much or singled out for favorable attention.

ESFPs notice everything, picking up subtleties that escape most people. They identify nuances in situations before others know what's happening. They're equally sensitive to the physical aspects of their environment, such as slight changes in temperature, ambient sounds, and so on. For example, their enthusiasm about a formation of migrating geese may prompt them to point the sight out to others around them.

Their positive outlook on life often gives friends the impression that ESFPs lead a charmed existence even in the face of difficult situations. They have the gift of seeing the glass half-full and don't believe in bringing others down with their complaints. Their cheerful attitude helps them make the best of things. Downturns shouldn't be taken too seriously, they believe.

Because of their easy-going personalities and ability to get along with others, ESFPs often find themselves acting as peacemakers. Their effectiveness is based partly on their commitment to their personal values. They're concerned about the well-being of others, are keen observers of people's behaviors, and easily sense when things are going wrong. They desire to help in practical ways and respond quickly to the needs of others. ESFPs are good at helping friends, family and co-workers find solutions to conflicts. They might not be the best advice-givers around because they dislike theory and predicting the future. However, they're excellent at dealing with problems in concrete ways.

Falling in Love

ESFPs are likely to date a number of people until they find suitable long-term partners. If they think they've found the right person but start feeling uncomfortable about the relationship, they're unlikely to stick around. They prefer to leave before the other one does, as they're deeply hurt by rejection. When a partner shows that he or she is loyal and dependable, they warm up and are generous with their affection.

ESFPs display their attachment in many ways—offering compliments, bringing gifts, and so on. Sometimes they can overwhelm their partners, making them feel inadequate to respond in kind. Or their demonstrations of love may be so extravagant that lovers start to withdraw when they weary of the excessive attention.

If the relationship turns sour and ends, ESFPs seldom harbor ill will toward the ex-partner. They're quick to move on. However, they do welcome the support of valued friends as they get back on their feet again.

At Work

ESFPs enjoy careers that involve action and working among productive, easy-going colleagues. They need plenty of opportunities to interact with others—co-workers, customers, and so on. Serving as a resource to people is an important motivator for ESFPs and helps make their jobs fulfilling. The atmosphere of their work setting is crucial to their career satisfaction.

When crises arise, ESFPs are quick to react. They focus on immediate solutions and encourage others to collaborate in solving problems. This leadership style promotes good will and teamwork in the work environment. While ESFPs are more people-oriented than task-oriented, they're quite capable of doing their jobs independently if the working atmosphere is positive.

As leaders, they're good at motivating co-workers. They're skilled at sizing up the potential of people and lining them up with the right resources. Their upbeat attitude and sociable natures make them effective goodwill ambassadors for their organizations.

Home Life

ESFPs are devoted to their families. They're good with children, treating them as equals. They play games and hold discussions that can be almost adult in tone. Whether the activities involve crafts projects, sporting events, or dinners out, they enjoy spending time with their partners and children.

Although they take pleasure in family events, ESFPs are not good planners when it comes to holiday celebrations, birthdays and anniversaries. Time management is not their long suit. They tend to move from one activity to the next without finishing any of them. When this puts them in a bad light with family members, they try to make amends.

Growing Older

In retirement, ESFPs continue their action-oriented lives. They fill their days with activities that involve other people. They maintain old friendships and continue to provide amusing company as they have in the past. Their energy is contagious.

Because ESFPs are so action-oriented and live in the "now," they may not plan adequately for their retirement years. Without enough resources, they can be at a loss for where to turn. Family members and friends can encourage them to anticipate the realities of retirement ahead of time. Fortunately, others are usually willing to help the ESFP in need, as people of this personality type make many valued friends over the years.

Chapter 10

ESTJ—The Supervisor

Extraverted, Sensing, Thinking, and Judging

Decisive	*Direct*
Clear	*Organized*
Objective	*Responsible*
Hard-working	*Impersonal*

*E*STJs are natural organizers—dependable, practical, and competent at whatever they undertake. They develop plans of action based on logic and prior experience and then roll up their sleeves to participate in the work. They monitor progress to make sure everything is done on time.

ESTJs are at their best solving concrete problems with visible outcomes. Abstract thinking is difficult for them. From their point of view, it's often pointless.

ESTJs are sociable, courteous, and appropriate in their behavior. They're fun to be with when they're not caught up in managing situations. When asked to take charge of projects, they usually say yes because they like being in control and enjoy the responsibility. They're free with their opinions, whether others agree with them or not. Some people find them too direct.

Falling in Love

When ESTJs fall in love, they set aside their usual matter-of-fact behavior. They become spontaneous—surprisingly receptive to whatever the moment offers. As a relationship progresses, however, they return to their more realistic, direct manner of behaving.

ESTJs are loyal to their partners, rarely yielding to flirtations with others. They offer emotional security in a relationship and expect the same in return. When a partner strays, the ESTJ is highly upset—not understanding how this could happen. If the partner is doubtful about their relationship and suggests a separation, the ESTJ may overreact and think that it's all over. Instead of trying to negotiate areas of disagreement and salvage the partnership, the ESTJ is likely to believe that there's no way to repair the harm done.

ESTJs tend to play conventional gender roles in relationships, doing what they think is expected of them. They are traditionalists. The ESTJ man pays for dinners out and theatre tickets. The ESTJ woman dresses attractively to please her date, or prepares a dinner for two in her apartment. Even though the female ESTJ has the same control needs as the male ESTJ, she will follow her partner's lead in social situations if it seems the accepted thing to do.

At Work

ESTJs whose careers are compatible with their personalities often stay on their jobs for years. As long as their needs are met and they continue being promoted, they see no need to look for greener fields. They don't want to take chances on risky moves that might not turn out well.

ESTJs prefer work that's structured and has clear objectives. It's important for them to know the specific requirements of projects and what the deadlines are. Problems may arise when ESTJs are given assignments without fully grasping their underlying purpose. They can get lost in details and veer off course without intending to.

At work, ESTJs respect the organization's hierarchy and reporting system. Because they tend to take charge of situations quickly, they often rise to positions of leadership. However, in their zeal to accomplish things, ESTJs may not develop personal relationships at work and appear cold to colleagues. With their crisp personal manner, they sometimes neglect to offer words of encouragement to co-workers. While they'll listen to subordinates' opinions, they expect everyone to abide by their final decision. Because they rely on logic so much, they may overlook niceties such as "please" and "thank you."

Home Life

Because work comes before pleasure, family members can expect limited leisure time with ESTJs. Household chores, homework, and social obligations must be taken care of first. Even then, ESTJs prefer leisure activities with a purpose. Going for walks is not for pure enjoyment. It's usually associated with losing weight or giving family members time to talk together.

ESTJ parents live orderly domestic lives. They make lists and schedules. Their children are expected to obey the rules and live up to the parents' expectations. There is little room for spontaneous fun or frivolity. If the children are out with their ESTJ parent on errands and there's a list to follow, their pleas to stop at the ice cream store are likely to be ignored.

ESTJs seldom mix work with family activities. Work stays at the office and is kept separate from home life. Parenting responsibilities and personal leisure are treated separately, too—with family obligations taking priority. Because they are so dependable and conscientious, ESTJs are often regarded as pillars of the community.

Growing Older

The transition to retirement can be difficult for ESTJs whose working lives have been invested in important, responsible careers. Unless they have set the stage for personal activities during retirement, they may find the sudden change hard to accept and even become susceptible to bouts of depression.

Many ESTJ retirees adjust by continuing to make lists and schedules based on different sets of agendas. Volunteer work, outings with friends and family, and hobbies may occupy much of the time that was once taken up by work.

Chapter 11

ESTP—The Promoter

Extraverted, Sensing, Thinking, and Perceiving

Adaptable	*Spontaneous*
Versatile	*Practical*
Energetic	*Easy-going*
Alert	*Persuasive*

*E*STPs are quick-thinking, action-oriented people. They're outgoing, lively, and entertaining. ESTPs can be found where the action is, joining in with whatever is happening. They're at their best dealing with situations that call for a no-nonsense, hands-on approach. In the company of others, they're direct with their comments, mincing no words.

ESTPs are risk takers, whether the risks are physical, financial or intellectual. They're willing to play for high stakes in the hope of high rewards. They especially enjoy looking for loopholes or unusual pay-offs relative to the time or money invested. While they know how to play by the rules, they sometimes ignore them to get what they want. They study all the angles of a situation before they act.

When things get too routine in the ESTP's life, he or she may take up hang gliding, white-water rafting or other high-risk sport that requires quick thinking. Attacking the unpredictable gives them a rush.

Falling in Love

For ESTPs, love has less to do with physical intimacy and romance than it does with finding a fun partner with whom to share life's adventures. When ESTPs find such a person, they will go to great lengths to impress him or her. To them, winning an exciting partner is a challenge that they can't resist. In their opinion, this is the object of romance. Generally, ESTPs are not creative or passionate lovers, although they enjoy physical intimacy.

ESTPs don't take romance as seriously as they do exciting, risk-taking ventures. If their daily life gets too routine, they'll invent new experiences to share with the partner—a trip abroad or an extravagant gift such as a new car. In this way, they offer a tangible symbol of their love while giving both partners a bold new undertaking to enjoy.

If a partner breaks up with them, they may suffer for some time, but before long they decide that life is too short for grief and sadness. They cut their losses and face reality. It's as though they've been through an illness. Once it's over, it's time to move on.

At Work

ESTPs put a lot of emphasis on their careers for fulfillment in life. Ideally, they seek positions where the work involves risk-taking and high rewards. On the job, they can be counted on to make things happen quickly. They're willing to undertake new ventures, tackle crises, and dive in to solve them.

Employees can rely on ESTPs to provide realistic assessments of what's going on in the workplace, what factual information is needed to proceed effectively, and how to handle matters the most efficient way. The sooner ESTPs can work their way through a problem, the happier they are. Then they can take on something new.

ESTPs prefer jobs that deal with realities, not abstract theories. They want to know "what is," not "what might be." Only information of current use is of much interest to them. They need concrete expectations, with detailed outcomes and deadlines.

Home Life

ESTPs are fun to live with, given their spontaneity and practical orientation to life. They know how to antic-ipate the needs of partners and children when it suits them. Sometimes, though, they're so blunt and direct that their families take offense because ESTPs can overlook ordinary courtesies. They may need help curbing their high energy to avoid overwhelming others. Sometimes they're outrageous on purpose and have to be told that it's not appreciated.

ESTPs tend to live in cluttered home environments because they have so much going on at once—much of it requiring various kinds of paraphernalia. However, specific areas of the house may be organized enough to let them find the right thing when it's needed. When asked where a certain item is, the ESTP can generally lead the person straight to it. The parts of their home that are orderly usually relate to their hobbies or special interests.

As parents, ESTPs have realistic expectations. They don't need their children to make A's in school as long as they're applying themselves and working toward some-thing that makes them happy.

Growing Older

While ESTPs calm down somewhat in retirement, they retain much of their vigor, curiosity, and sense of adventure. They continue to need to test their minds and bodies. Otherwise, retirement would be drudgery. They enjoy their grandchildren, taking them on trips and going to concerts, sports events, and other fun outings.

Some ESTPs retire early so they have more opportunity for fun. In search of adventure, they look for others to share the excitement with them. While they're not joiners at heart and dislike leading, they may look for groups that pave the way to new travel experiences, physical activities, hobbies, and so on. Their loyalty to groups depends on whether they're having fun. They can move in and out of organizations at any time.

Chapter 12

INFJ—The Counselor

Introverted, Intuitive, Feeling, and Judging

Compassionate	*Sensitive*
Intense	*Idealistic*
Creative	*Loyal*
Reserved	*Determined*

*I*NFJs are kind, generous, and supportive of others. If someone needs help, they're there for them. People with problems can rely on INFJs to suggest creative solutions or offer hands-on support.

The integrity of INFJs is evident in everything they do in the workplace, at home, and in the community. Their actions reflect their ideals. They're not outspoken about their principles, preferring to make them apparent in the things they do. This is partly due to their need for privacy and desire to avoid the spotlight. They do their best thinking in solitude where they can concentrate on their ideas and inspiration without interruption.

When INFJs set their minds on a goal, they're persistent and even stubborn. If they encounter resistance, it only makes them more determined. They have a quiet strength that is respected by those around them. INFJs often benefit from spending time with friends who are more outgoing. Extraverts encourage them to share their inventive ideas and put them into action.

INFJs are keen observers of group dynamics, able to sense undercurrents and detect the motives of others. It's hard to put much over on an INFJ.

Falling in Love

When INFJs feel a romantic attachment, they may make subtle gestures to encourage displays of affection from the other person. At the same time, they are somewhat cautious about expressing their own feelings for fear of rejection. Some people find them aloof because they do such a good job of concealing their caring nature. They have a hard time making their needs known. For partners who realize this and have the patience to fish for clues, INFJs eventually reveal their personalities.

INFJs are rewarding companions because they have rich imaginations and agile minds. They inspire their partners to grow and develop. They don't try to control others.

Because of their need to be loved, INFJs may get involved in relationships that aren't always right for them. When they suspect this, they often continue the partnership because the intimacy is so important to them. If another, more suitable partner comes along, they usually end the failing relationship to pursue the new love. In this, they are focused and intense.

INFJs whose partners break up with them tend to be devastated and deal with the crisis by looking for their own mistakes and shortcomings. They suffer a period of lowered self-esteem. Without others to help them overcome their grief, they're slow to regroup their energies and move on.

INFJs often have unrealistic expectations of what makes an ideal relationship. If they fail to adjust their dreams to reality and find flaws in a partner, they may start looking elsewhere for intimacy without making an effort to work out their differences.

At Work

INFJs seek careers that allow them to preserve their values and serve others. While they collaborate well with co-workers, they're capable of doing most projects independently. With colleagues, they are personable, easy-going, and dependable. They can be counted on to meet their commitments. They also help others reach their goals, providing generous counsel and hands-on help.

While INFJs take pleasure in their jobs, they're averse to conflicts and stress in the workplace. When these arise, they can become rigid and uncommunicative. Conflict resolution is not their long suit.

Home Life

INFJs are idealists, nowhere more so than in their own homes. They desire harmony above all—sometimes sidestepping family conflicts that should be resolved for the good of everyone.

As parents, INFJs give their children every opportunity for a good education and the development of life skills. INFJs are tolerant of differences and idiosyncrasies as long as their children put forth genuine effort. INFJs share their time and resources generously with their kids.

INFJs' homes usually contain an abundance of books, articles, crafts supplies, musical instruments, and other paraphernalia that allow them to follow their interests and hobbies. The more they can share these with family members, the happier they are. At the same time, they need space of their own where they can work privately.

Sometimes the homes of INFJs are neat and organized. Sometimes they're not. Keeping their environment in order feels good but doesn't take priority. When partners and children complain that the INFJs work areas are a mess, he or she will try to tidy up. Their surroundings may be cluttered but their minds are extremely organized. Their inner lives take priority.

Growing Older

INFJs enjoy their retirement years if they have enough leisure time to pursue their dreams. After decades of hard work, they're able to set aside many of the world's problems that once consumed them with worry. They've reached a stage where they figure it's the next generation's problem.

All sorts of creative projects may surface that couldn't be undertaken while the INFJ was still employed. Many INFJs read to their heart's content for the first time in their lives. Because they're so articulate, some turn to creative or nonfiction writing. Without the pressure of earning a paycheck, they can indulge in activities that allow them to express themselves.

Chapter 13

INFP—The Healer

Introverted, Intuitive, Feeling, and Perceiving

Gentle	*Quiet*
Loyal	*Curious*
Honest	*Adaptable*
Creative	*Compassionate*

*I*NFPs are soft-spoken idealists who dedicate themselves to helping others. Their strong value system guides their choices in life. Although they live by self-imposed codes, they don't burden others with their beliefs. They avoid conflict and try not to create waves by telling others what to do. They make exceptions when they see people behaving cruelly, unfairly, or dishonestly. Then they become surprisingly assertive, even aggressive.

People are sometimes confused by the inconsistency of this behavior. How can such quiet, polite individuals suddenly break into harsh words with others? INFPs are only abiding by their logical, deeply rooted code of honor.

INFPs have rich inner lives and treasure their solitude. Their intuition is highly developed, giving them the ability to see what's going on under the surface. They understand why people do the things they do. Because they can see through facades and games, deceivers and players can seldom fool them for long. They examine every piece of evidence for its fundamental truth and then seek the wider context into which it fits.

INFPs set such high standards for themselves that they're often disappointed in the results of their work. As a result, they're somewhat prone to depression. Their introversion inclines them to be loners, giving them the tendency to brood over problems without checking the facts with others. Their feeling preference often causes them to exaggerate the importance of conflicts or hurt feelings.

Falling in Love

INFPs are idealists about romance. Many won't settle for partners who seem less than perfect. When INFPs get frustrated in their search for such a person, they become disheartened and may avoid dating opportunities for a while.

When an INFP does find a partner, he or she is likely to arrange the details of their relationship to create perfect intimacy—a cozy corner of an ethnic restaurant for dinners out, a gift of jewelry that has been in the family, a fine wine, and so on. The details aren't as important as the personal investment in the relationship.

INFPs are shy about expressing themselves, sometimes leaving their partners uncertain about where they stand. Since INFPs need to hear expressions of affection themselves, one would think they'd recognize it in others. They have a hard time asking for reassurances of love.

When their relationships run into trouble, INFPs may have difficulty discussing problems openly with their partners. They're not likely to talk with friends, either. If a partner breaks up with them, they are deeply hurt and go through a period of withdrawal. Afterward they may overreact, feeling anger toward the partner. It's hard for them to accept the end of a relationship.

At Work

INFPs do best with co-workers who share their work ethics and values. When they see colleagues working at cross-purposes or sabotaging each other, it disturbs them deeply. They want everyone to cooperate for the general good and are suspicious of competition.

Open communication with colleagues is not the long suit of INFPs. At work they may need prompting to share the details of what they're doing and what progress they're making on various projects. Still, people usually enjoy working with them.

Privacy and quiet are important to INFPs as they work. They need an environment where they can think about what they're doing without interruption. Bureaucratic details try their patience.

Home Life

At home, INFPs are gentle and easy-going. While they're generally predictable, they can surprise their families by changing direction suddenly. Often the reason for the change is that they're trying to be better partners or parents. A father who once looked down on team sports may volunteer to be a soccer coach at school when his child joins a team. A mother who always avoided traditional feminine roles may start baking cookies for her child's grade school class.

INFPs usually have more home projects under way than they can complete. Their work areas are likely to be piled with books, crafts projects, home improvement tools, and so on. While they may intend to follow through in a disciplined way, their self-imposed schedules fall apart. Instead, family life takes priority. They want to keep everyone happy. Many chores are left undone, including picking up after themselves and keeping things tidy.

INFP parents are warm and affirming. They make good confidantes for their children. However, they have a tendency to avoid problems and unpleasant issues, which can sow the seeds for poor communication and misunderstandings.

Growing Older

Retirement is enjoyable for INFPs because they know how to entertain themselves. After a lifetime of work, they take pleasure in having time to reflect, read, and share leisure time with loved ones. In the company of others, they're charming and entertaining. Their sense of humor keeps everyone smiling. At the same time, INFPs are good at respecting the privacy of intimates because they understand this need so well.

Retired INFPs may short-change themselves by putting off important projects because they're too busy looking after the rest of the family. It's important for them to share their dreams openly because they may need encouragement to follow through on long-postponed activities such as travel.

Chapter 14

INTJ—The Mastermind

Introverted, Intuitive, Thinking, and Judging

Consistent	*Critical*
Rational	*Independent*
Reticent	*Creative*
Future-oriented	*Knowledgeable*

*I*NTJs are one of the most independent Myers-Briggs types. Sometimes they seem so confident that people find them overbearing. Because INTJs like to debate issues, they're often accused of being argumentative. When told this, INTJs can be stunned and hurt. That wasn't their intention. They see themselves as encouraging improvement in others.

People of this personality type are good organizers. As a result, they often rise to leadership positions. With their strong intuition, they're good at seeing the big picture and solving problems. They're skilled at planning projects and approaching tasks efficiently. They don't walk away from projects and leave the details to others. Instead, they collaborate with teammates to bring the work to completion.

To INTJs the world is rich in possibilities. They feel that there's always room for improvement and they feel qualified to lead the way.

Falling in Love

When INTJs find a new lover, they want to include the person in every aspect of their lives. Usually, the partners they choose have the qualities they've been seeking all along. They know what they want in a mate and how they want the relationship to function. An INTJ woman who spends much of her time outdoors camping and hiking looks for a partner with similar interests. No matter how attractive a bookish academic person may appear, she won't feel a connection. A man who makes his living as a concert violinist won't find much appeal in a follower of punk rock.

The affections of INTJs are expressed more in what they do than what they say. They have trouble talking about their deep feelings, even with a romantic partner. Instead, they buy expensive gifts their partners will appreciate. An INTJ man whose partner is an art lover may buy him or her an expensive painting. A woman involved with a partner who enjoys winter sports may buy cross-country skis as a gift.

If a relationship starts to fall apart, the INTJ is likely to withdraw and remain silent about his or her feelings, even with the partner. Also, INTJs tend to assume that there's a right and a wrong way to end a relationship, and they want to do it properly. Outwardly they may seem unaffected by the break-up, but the chances are that they're suffering.

At Work

INTJs prefer careers that let them express their creativity and change the way things work. They like to design models based on theories they've developed and see their visions become a reality. They prefer projects that can be approached in an organized way as they work with a good deal of autonomy. They dislike micromanagement.

As highly determined types, INTJs follow every step they've formulated to reach their goals. When others disagree with their plans or suggest more practical goals, INTJs are surprised and dismayed. They don't understand why people don't appreciate their models.

While they benefit from support and encouragement, INTJs often neglect to show appreciation for the ideas and accomplishments of fellow workers. Also, they sometimes lack empathy and need to express their feelings more openly.

Home Life

INTJs may intimidate their partners and children without realizing it. Their style is not warm and fuzzy. They tend to be impersonal about disagreements, acting as though they don't care about the opinions of others. They're surprised when they learn that they make family members uncomfortable. Their independent outlook may make their partners and children hesitate to challenge them.

INTJs, always looking for a way to improve their lives, need to encourage family members to express their own opinions rather than assuming that everybody in the family agrees with them. They need to show respect for the things others in the family say and do.

INTJs tend to develop models of ideal behavior in their minds, applying them to others as well as themselves. An INTJ father may decide what college would be best for his son and what his major should be, failing to consider the boy's preferences and personality. A mother who is a biologist may not understand the needs of a daughter who wants to be a musician because it doesn't fit her idea of what a child should study in college.

When vacation time comes, the children of INTJ parents shouldn't expect to spend their time lolling on the beach. For INTJs, leisure time should have a purpose. If a beach is the family's destination, the chances are that many productive activities will be included on the agenda.

Growing Older

As INTJs approach retirement, they may become less driven and more willing to enjoy immediate pleasures. They relax their need for improvement in themselves and others. By transforming their abstract ideas into productive hobbies and enjoyable social activities, they can cultivate the sensing and feeling functions that they've neglected for years and start living in the present more than the future. Family members may find them more relaxed and accessible.

Chapter 15

INTP—The Problem Solver

Introverted, Intuitive, Thinking, and Perceiving

Rational	*Independent*
Detached	*Intellectual*
Skeptical	*Speculative*
Reticent	*Exacting*

*I*NTPs are intensely private. They need time alone to explore the creative possibilities arising from their well-developed intuition. Their ability to absorb new information seems endless. Their objective thinking requires that all incoming data be analyzed for accuracy and tested against their existing theories about reality.

INTPs strive for perfection in the way they think. In their world, ideas can always be improved upon. Sometimes this attitude is self-punishing, as the INTP brain never seems able to stop its intellectual efforts.

Falling in Love

Falling in love is a "head over heels" event, even if it lasts only a few months. It seems like a tidal wave that carries INTPs on its crest, over which they have little control. During this stage, they're likely to write poetry, buy special gifts, and question the new partner about every aspect of his or her life. They tend to overlook all flaws in the person. They will move mountains to be together at every opportunity.

The period of infatuation is followed by the return of their more familiar style of privacy and reticence. Expressions of affection are offered less frequently. Exchanges with the partner become more matter of fact. This doesn't mean that INTPs no longer take their commitment seriously. Because the relationship seems so stable to them, they assume their partner feels the same way.

Falling out of love happens when INTPs see that their expectations were unrealistic. Once that occurs, the end is in sight. While the initial break-up is usually amicable, long-term effects can result and all the parties involved may suffer. If the couple continues to have important things in common, the relationship may continue, but on a different basis.

At Work

INTPs prefer careers that involve logic and structured thinking. They're good at abstract thought and the construction of models. They're likely to continue working on a project as long as the problem-solving process remains challenging. Once they lose interest in the possibilities, they may find it hard to stay motivated. They prefer thinking about how something should be fixed than actually rolling up their sleeves and fixing it.

If there are guidelines and rules about how to proceed with tasks, INTPs aren't likely to follow them. They'd rather devise their own ways of doing things. Also, they like to work on their own timetable, not on schedules imposed by others.

Home Life

INTPs can be unpredictable in their family roles because they're always open to new ways of doing things. They expect that other family members will welcome their novel ideas and innovations. To them, the prospect of change is challenging and exciting.

The INTP father who, in his daughter's grade school years, made trips to the library and read books with her every night, may be surprised by her sudden interest in sports when she reaches middle school. Rather than feel disappointed, the father is excited by this new phase of her development and volunteers to be an after-school coach at his daughter's school.

Home projects are exciting for INTPs but the most enjoyable part is making lists of tasks to be done and supplies to be purchased. Collecting information and drawing up plans is what they're best at. Carrying projects through to completion is another matter. This can frustrate family members who were looking forward to the finished work.

INTPs like to debate issues at the dinner table, a habit that may irritate less competitive family members. Because intellectual activity is so important to INTPs, they like to challenge the ideas of others. The family, on the other hand, may prefer amiable conversation. When INTPs get too wrapped up in the excitement of arguing, they may seem downright rude to their partners and children.

At home, periods of privacy are of paramount importance to INTPs. They regroup their energies when they're alone. The family needs to give them ample time to read, think, spend time on their computer, and so on.

Growing Older

INTPs often need the encouragement of family and friends to stay connected with other people during retirement. It's too easy for them to spend all their time alone. Often, games requiring thought and strategy are good social outlets. Bridge, poker and chess give INTPs the risk-taking opportunities they enjoy and don't require small talk or attention to meaningless details. Most important, they engage the strategic, problem-solving abilities of the brain while providing the INTP with social interaction.

Retirement is a time when many INTPs expand their use of unfamiliar Myers-Briggs functions. Instead of relying exclusively on their intuition, they start to engage their sensing function in ways such as playing an instrument, painting, or enjoying outdoor activities. Their feeling function may be re-activated by activities shared with family members.

Chapter 16

ISFJ—The Protector

Introverted, Sensing, Feeling, and Judging

Modest	*Down-to-earth*
Easy-going	*Orderly*
Helpful	*Caring*
Practical	*Dependable*

*I*SFJs are modest, orderly and easy-going but have a strong sense of duty. They put much of their energy into helping others. People can count on them in times of trouble. They're practical and down-to-earth in everything they do. They rely on the "now" to guide their thinking and behavior. They're not much concerned about the future.

With little need to control others, the main desire of ISFJs is to see everyone living in harmony. Their respect extends to animals and the environment. They have a hard time understanding people who need power. ISFJs are bewildered by greed and unkindness because it's foreign to their natures. They are so wary of being intrusive that they often deprive the world of their creativity and practical skills.

ISFJs tend to be more cautious and shy than their friends and may make up white lies to avoid being criticized. An ISFJ who doesn't drink alcohol, for example, may have a hard time resisting social pressure. Instead of saying, "I don't drink," he or she may say, "I'm allergic to alcohol."

They usually have only a few close friends, people they may have known for a lifetime. They don't join many social groups, but often belong to at least one. ISFJs contribute in quiet, practical ways, avoiding center stage. Others value them for their kindness and friendliness. The gentleness of ISFJs may cause them to be overlooked or overpowered by others. In a way, they are the least visible of the sixteen Myers-Briggs types.

Falling in Love

ISFJs take their relationships seriously. They're attentive to their partners' needs and ready to do helpful favors. Their loyalty and steadfast commitment may be expressed in such subtle ways that they seem overly serious. This can be annoying to partners who prefer a more carefree lifestyle.

Because of their reliable nature, ISFJs often lay aside their personal career ambitions to accommodate a partner in some way—moving to another location, changing jobs, etc. They find it hard to speak up for their own needs. In fact, they're inclined to let more assertive partners ride roughshod over them.

ISFJs hesitate to leave relationships, even when they're no longer working. When a romance goes wrong and a partner shows signs of calling the whole thing off, ISFJs grow quiet and hide their distress in an effort to appear composed and stoic to the people around them.

At Work

ISFJs are hard workers and like to see the results of their efforts, knowing that they've made a difference in people's lives. They expect their jobs to be fun and satisfying and are attracted to occupations that require dedication to others.

ISFJs need careers that are consistent with their values and satisfy their desire to serve others. They're happier with conventional careers that focus on short-term goals and hands-on attention to detail than those that require long-range planning and problem-solving.

ISFJs dislike conflicts and stress in the workplace. However, if a job disappointments them, ISFJs are likely to keep trying, working harder in the hope of improving matters. For them, work is a source of inspiration. Unless they see the difference they've made in the world around them, they don't feel fulfilled.

Home Life

ISFJs take on many chores and responsibilities, sometimes more than they can handle. They may complain about their workload in a martyred sort of way, but if others try to help, they are likely to turn down their offers. When family members do lend a hand, the ISFJ may feel inadequate and guilty.

Celebrations such as birthdays and anniversaries are important to ISFJs, giving them a chance to support family traditions. To enjoy themselves, however, they must participate fully in the preparations—perhaps cooking the holiday meal, cleaning the house for visitors, and so on. This is how they show their commitment and love.

As parents they take their jobs seriously. They see parenting as a lifelong commitment. Protective and patient with their children, they often set aside their own priorities in favor of meeting their children's needs.

Growing Older

As ISFJs mature, they're less hard on themselves. They become more extraverted, make new friends, and put more emphasis on leisure activities. Their personal desires take higher priority than they did in the past. Still, for them to be happy, retirement must be filled with purpose and service to others.

As grandparents, they're likely to give grandchildren anything they want. They'll take them places, buy clothes for them, and even make sure their education is paid for. Grandchildren soon learn that their generosity can be counted on.

Chapter 17

ISFP—The Artist

Introverted, Sensing, Feeling, and Perceiving

Compassionate	*Perceptive*
Gentle	*Observant*
Modest	*Loyal*
Adaptable	*Spontaneous*

*I*SFPs are more in touch with themselves and the world around them than most other types. They are driven by a love of life and a desire to see and know about everything. Their natural curiosity makes them as interested in the natural world as in people.

ISFPs are driven by the need to encourage others to fulfill their potential while not intruding or imposing on them. Because of their gentle, compassionate nature, they may find that other, more assertive types overlook their contributions. Being somewhat shy, they may not appreciate their own accomplishments and skills. In fact, their inner voices are often too critical. When ISFPs are able to share their feelings, friends and colleagues may succeed in convincing them that they have more assets than they realize.

Because of their kind, tactful nature, ISFPs sometimes take responsibility for issues that belong to others in order to keep the peace. They need encouragement to be honest and open, as it creates a path to better relationships in the future.

ISFPs are often graceful and athletic. They enjoy the feeling of their bodies in motion and have a physical awareness of what they can and cannot do. They can excel at physical activities requiring both sensitivity and strength, such as dancing and figure skating.

Falling in Love

Falling in love is a major event for ISFPs. In the first stages of a love affair, they are consumed by delight. They set aside future worries in order to immerse themselves in the new relationship. Once committed, they make devoted, loyal partners, always considering the needs of their lovers. They find many ways to show their appreciation for the other person. They may even change careers, move, or make other major life changes for the partner.

In their desire to please their partners, ISFPs may fail to stand up for their own needs. When rejected, they withdraw and rehash every aspect of the relationship in their minds, wondering where they went wrong. They tend to assume more of the blame than is warranted. Friends can help them face reality, encourage them to become more assertive, and motivate them to resume their normal lives.

ISFPs who are unfortunate enough to have self-serving or manipulative partners are exposed to considerable potential harm because of their natural vulnerability and self-critical tendencies.

At Work

ISFPs acquire job skills best through hands-on experience. They have little interest in knowledge acquired through theoretical or abstract approaches, preferring to learn in applied ways. They're also averse to bureaucratic structures that deprive them of their spontaneity and freedom. They want to learn in settings relevant to their job assignments.

ISFPs often choose careers where they function quietly behind the scenes, helping others. While generally quiet and gentle, they can be remarkably persuasive if they believe in their course of action. When they think that a situation demands an immediate, assertive response, they are often surprisingly outspoken. Under these conditions, they have little need to impress others with their tact.

ISFPs are generally a pleasure to work with. Because their outlook is basically humanistic, they are always concerned about the well being of others. They particularly enjoy co-workers who, like them, are flexible and compatible. Their upbeat attitude and cooperative nature foster a collegial atmosphere in the workplace.

ISFPs do best in environments they can personalize by making them aesthetically pleasing. Privacy is an important factor because of their preference for introversion.

ISFPs generally avoid leadership roles unless the situation demands it. However, they're ready to come forward in emergencies, doing whatever is needed. When they do assume leadership, their approach is egalitarian. They're good at motivating others through praise and encouragement.

Home Life

ISFPs invest themselves fully in their homes and relationships with family and friends. They are spontaneous and outgoing, accepting everyone they meet. Only when people are rude or mean, especially to those less fortunate, will ISFPs stand up assertively and show their disapproval. They are great advocates of victims' rights.

Because ISFPs are so quick to serve others, they may neglect their own needs. Over time, this can affect their morale and have a negative impact on their families. Family and friends can help by bringing them back to a more balanced view of their relationships with others.

Growing Older

Most ISFPs move into their retirement years with ease. They savor the opportunity to enjoy life moment by moment. Leisure time gives them the chance to share activities with people who are important to them. For example, they take special pleasure in surprising friends and family with tickets to special events or other amusing activities.

ISFPs are good at entertaining themselves, too. They often take up new hobbies such as carpentry, art, gourmet cooking, and outdoor sports. Having time to enjoy themselves alone, as well as with loved ones, is a special benefit of retirement.

Chapter 18

ISTJ—The Worker

Introverted, Sensing, Thinking, and Judging

Objective	*Practical*
Factual	*Organized*
Concrete	*Demanding*
Reliable	*Rule-bound*

*I*STJs are among the most responsible of Myers-Briggs types. They're also the most private. While they know how to be gracious and articulate in social situations, it's usually because they're trying to behave appropriately. Underneath the friendly facade, they remain introverts. They know how to mix and mingle, but they're most at home working independently or pursuing leisure activities alone.

ISTJs have a need to collect information before they take action on anything. They don't make impulsive decisions. They focus on concrete data, remembering the objective details of situations. They miss nothing and take nothing for granted. They're not comfortable with abstract ideas and complex intellectual activity.

Their qualities can make them demanding partners, parents and co-workers, because what they do naturally and easily is what they expect of everyone else. At times, their impatience can be hard to deal with.

Falling in Love

When ISTJs fall in love they make loyal partners. They aren't outwardly sentimental, however, and rarely express their feelings. To them, loyalty to their partners speaks louder than words. This can cause problems in a relationship when the partner feels ignored or unappreciated.

Because ISTJs are traditionalists at heart, they usually conform to stereotypes of their gender. Female ISTJs prefer conventional feminine roles, combining nurturing with their natural objective, organized natures. If the male partner of a female ISTJ is sick, she's at his bedside taking his temperature, bringing water and orange juice, and making sure he follows the doctor's instructions. ISTJ males are protective of their female partners in a "macho" sort of way. They know how to behave like the strong, commanding types our culture approves of—opening doors, pulling out chairs, and so on. As traditional types, they bring their partners candy and flowers on special occasions.

At Work

ISTJs gravitate toward careers that are practical and have tangible results. Jobs that allow them to work alone are especially attractive as long as they require objective problem-solving and produce concrete results. ISTJs prefer tasks they can do in prescribed ways, leaving little to invention. Surgery, law and accounting are examples of careers that attract ISTJs. They're less likely to be found in jobs that require abstract thinking. They dislike settings where much socializing is required. Spontaneous fun in groups of people makes the ISTJ anxious.

ISTJs like to play by the rules, and they want to work in a place where everyone else does, too. Free-wheeling is not acceptable. They expect colleagues to conform to their job descriptions and respect productivity as the prime goal of employment. Jobs that violate traditional boundaries make them uneasy. They may be uncomfortable with female surgeons, for example, or male nurses.

Home Life

ISTJs keep their home and yards neat. The house is decorated in a subdued, tasteful fashion. Things are put away. The modest, low-key interior reflects the reserve of the ISTJ personality. The yard is neat and orderly, too, with a few bushes and plants, but no extravagant landscaping. One doesn't see beds of flowers, exotic plant species, or even yard furniture.

ISTJs carry out their domestic duties promptly and efficiently. If Saturday is lawn-mowing day, the male ISTJ is out in the yard first thing that morning. If it's the day for grocery shopping, the female ISTJ will be headed out the door with an organized list.

Because they love tradition, ISTJs go all out to celebrate holidays and important family events. Birthdays and anniversaries require elaborate preparations. Everyone is expected to show up and participate. Those who fail to do so are likely to have a guilt trip laid on them.

ISTJ parents make rules and regulations for their children. Whatever the ISTJ learned while growing up is passed down to his or her offspring. Family roles are clear. Mothers and fathers make the rules and children follow them. Children have jobs to do, just as the grown-ups do. Even leisure time tends to be scheduled.

Growing Older

ISTJs can surprise friends and family in their retirement years. ISTJs who were once demanding and difficult may loosen up. They may become more spontaneous and fun-loving with friends and family.

A classic example of the ISTJ whose personality softens in retirement is the grandmother who was once a firm disciplinarian with her children only to become playful and easy-going with her grandchildren. A tough executive entering retirement may surprise everyone by turning his home office into a music studio, complete with stereo recording equipment.

Chapter 19

ISTP—The Artisan

Introverted, Sensing, Thinking, and Perceiving

Independent	*Analytical*
Sensible	*Adventurous*
Logical	*Skillful*
Factual	*Enterprising*

*A*s observers of life, ISTPs don't miss much. They're logical and adaptable to existing circumstances. They do well in situations that require immediate action.

Whether at work or play, they enjoy activities that require hands-on skills. They collect details about subjects that interest them. If they're baseball fans, they know the statistics about players. If they're nature enthusiasts, they can tell you the genus and species of wildflowers, birds, and so on.

Falling in Love

When ISTPs fall in love, they show their affection with favors and small gifts rather than romantic words. They aren't good at talking about their feelings. They think their actions should speak for themselves. In written communication such as e-mails, they're often unclear. The partner wonders what they're driving at.

ISTPs like to share their interests and hobbies with partners. Conversations with their partners often don't concern the relationship at all. They're more likely to involve the details of leisure activities or events at work. An ISTP can go on and on about camping gear, how they set up a project at work, or the features of different car models. Sometimes these discussions are boring for partners who prefer to talk about more personal matters.

If a relationship is failing, ISTPs often feel helpless to do much about it. It's hard for them to explore their own painful feelings or listen to a partner's. They tend to ignore unpleasant realities and continue as they were, giving up hope only when the evidence tells them that it's useless to continue. Then they take a stoic attitude, no matter what pain they're feeling inside, and simply move on.

At Work

ISTPs like jobs with concrete objectives and clear tasks. They need to understand the practical goals of their projects. When approaching assignments, they look for the most efficient ways to get the job done and don't waste time on activities they regard as unimportant.

ISTPs are able to absorb complex details about technical systems and apply their knowledge in practical ways. Problem-solving is their long suit. When crises occur on the job, they can continue to work calmly even when the people around them are falling apart.

ISTPs are independent and inventive. They dislike being micromanaged and rebel under too many restrictions. They tend to be impersonal in their dealings with co-workers. It takes a long time for people to get to know them.

Under stress, ISTPs may take too many shortcuts at work and even slack off on the job. They may do the part of a project that's enjoyable and postpone less pleasant but critical steps.

Since ISTPs are generally reserved, they have a tendency to keep important details to themselves. They may not inform others about what's going on. Because diplomacy is not their strong point, they sometimes emphasize what others did wrong instead of what they did right. As a result, co-workers may view them as insensitive.

Home Life

ISTPs are generally neat at home. They keep their clothes put away and the kitchen counters cleared off. They like to work in a clean, orderly environment. Household projects interest ISTPs as long as they can work on their own schedule. They don't want to be rushed. This can be frustrating for partners and children who are waiting for the playroom to be painted. Someone waiting for an ISTP partner to mow the lawn may get frustrated watching the grass grow as the person stalls, doing more enjoyable things first.

Hobbies and leisure activities are important outlets for ISTPs. They'll spend whatever time and money are required to pursue them, even though they're not spend-thrifts at heart. When they get bored, they drop the old activities and move on to new ones.

While ISTPs amuse themselves easily on their own, they also enjoy sharing activities. They don't need to talk much, especially about abstract subjects or topics irrelevant to what they're doing. Their attention is focused on the present.

ISTPs encourage their children to share their interests, often involving them in practical ways. ISTP parents teach their children many skills and interests that will last a lifetime.

Growing Older

ISTPs look forward to retirement, especially if their work life was not fulfilling. They're finally able to pursue interests that they had to put off when they had full-time jobs. If their careers were challenging and rewarding, they may choose to continue employment in a modified way when they reach retirement age.

Because ISTPs are adventurous at heart, they may undertake completely new hobbies such as sailing, cross-country skiing, upholstering, or cake decorating. Able to indulge themselves fully in leisure pursuits for the first time, they can become completely engrossed. If they're financially secure, they're likely to spend money liberally on their new interests.

Chapter 20

What's Your Type?

*A*ccording to Myers-Briggs experts, no one personality type is better than the other. The types aren't set in stone. Not only can scores shift slightly from month to month depending on a person's circumstances, but they become more balanced with advancing age. In general, though, one preference in each of the four traits will dominate.

The Four Trait Pairs

Introvert (I) or Extravert (E)?
If your Myers-Briggs test reveals that you have a preference for introversion, you recharge your batteries by spending time alone or in the company of only one or two others. Groups of people wear you out after a while. On the other hand, if you're an extravert, you start getting

fidgety when you've had no social interaction for a while. You need people around you to stimulate and refresh you.

You're not locked into your energy preferences. Even introverts like to party sometimes, and extraverts need a little solitude now and then.

Sensing (S) or Intuitive (N)?

If your attention preference is sensing, you experience the world more through your five senses than through inner reflection. You believe in the tangible. Proof is everything. If, on the other hand, you are the intuitive type, you require less sensory data to draw conclusions. Instead, you reflect on the meaning of what's happening.

When two people attend a party and share observations in the car on the way home, the sensing type may say, "Did you see the diamond Jill was wearing?" The intuitive partner may answer, "No, but it's obvious that Jack is crazy about her."

Thinking (T) or Feeling (F)?

To reach personal decisions as a thinking type, you weigh the objective evidence and chart a course of action accordingly. As a feeling type, you consider how the decision fits into your value system and how it will affect others.

At work, a thinking supervisor may say, "If John doesn't improve his work output, I'll have to fire him."

The feeling supervisor may think, "John's work is below average, but he's struggling to keep two kids in college." Both are capable of reversing their opinion, given a little persuasion.

Perceiving (P) or Judging (J)?

Your preference for perceiving or judging determines your attitude toward life. As a judger, you think, "First things first." You pay your bills on time and meet your deadlines. A perceiving friend may be more open-ended. "Oh well, the bills can wait another month," or "If I don't make the deadline, no one is going to die."

That doesn't mean the judger isn't capable of taking off and going to the beach instead of working. The perceiver may think, "I'd better get this project done with time to spare or my job may be on the line," but then miss the next two deadlines.

Heredity vs. Environment

If you come from a family of shy people, the chances are you'll never be a booming extravert. You'll be shy, too. On the other hand, if you're an introvert in a family of extraverts where "survival of the loudest" is the rule, you may be forced to acquire social skills that help you live in this environment of outgoing individuals. However, your preference for introversion will always dominate.

Preferences are a little like left- and right-handedness. If you're right-handed, it's possible to write with your left hand, but not easy. When you're young you use your left hand only if both hands are required for a task, such as lifting a heavy object. Over the years, you learn to use your left hand more, particularly when you're trying to do two things at once. Taking notes with your right hand, you're able to drink coffee with your left. Some people are born ambidextrous. That is, they can perform tasks using either hand with equal skill. The ability to use some preferences equally is true of certain people, too, although it's the exception rather than the rule.

A person who once scored an almost perfect 9 on the introversion scale as a teenager may, by age 50, score 6 and 3 on the introversion and extraversion scales, respectively. This can be compared to right-handed people continuing to use their right hand to write checks, but learning to make more use of their left hand to perform other tasks. The shift is part of maturing and making the most of one's abilities. The introvert who would rather read a book than go to a party may say, "I think I'll go anyhow. It will be good for me." The person is trying to say, "I need to stretch my boundaries and become more balanced."

Balance

A balanced person uses all eight preferences, calling upon each when it's needed. A homebody may be happy spending most of the day alone but look forward to evenings out with friends. A sensing husband whose wife comes home late several nights in a row may intuit that she's been having an affair. A cool-headed father of the thinking type may insist that his teenage daughter meet midnight curfews, until she bursts into tears one night. When he finds that she's been invited to a graduation party, he softens and relents. A judging type may have a work deadline looming but then decide, the heck with it, I'm going to a movie.

Is it best to develop all the functions equally? According to Carl Jung, the Swiss psychoanalyst who developed personality theory, the answer is no. If a person dedicates a period of his or her life to, say, sensing and intuition simultaneously, neither function will get the attention and energy needed to become fully developed. The same is true of the other three trait pairs. One of each pair of functions must be dominant at any given time to produce a stable, reliable personality.

The goal of personal development in terms of the Myers-Briggs theory is to have access to each of the personality functions when its use is appropriate. By being able to use the less-preferred functions when they are needed, the person brings more balance to his or her life.

Cultural Influence and Prevalence

The Myers-Briggs test is now a standard psychological test in more than 25 countries around the world. All sixteen types appear in all cultures studied so far. People of different cultures use the test for similar reasons: to help them plan their careers, improve their business relationships, and promote personal development.

Three personality types predominate in all cultures: sensing, thinking, and judging. Sensing types depend on concrete facts to form their perceptions of the world and make decisions. They don't trust hunches. Thinking types are rational. They, too, use facts to make decisions—leaning away from emotional issues because they don't trust them as much as facts. Judging types like closure and completion. They make decisions promptly and finish things on time.

Only the introverted and extraverted types show significant differences in their prevalence in various cultures. Great Britain, for example, has more introverts than extraverts, while the opposite is true in the United States. In the U.S., extraversion is considered an asset. This isn't true in the U.K., where introversion is more the norm.

INFJs—the rarest type—make up only 1 percent of the world population. Other low-end groups include INTJs, ENTPs, ENFJs, and ENTJs at 2 to 5 percent each. The most heavily represented types are ISTJs, ISFJs, ISFPs, and ESFJs, at 9 to 14 percent. Combined, they account for almost half the population. Clustered around the middle are the other nine Myers Briggs types at 4 to 9 percent each. The prevalence rates of the 16 Myers-Briggs types worldwide are shown in the graph.

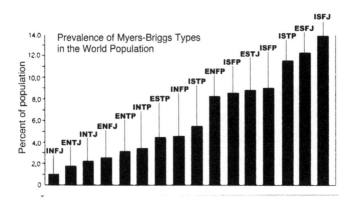

Learning More

Now that you've uncovered your hidden traits, encourage your friends and family to take the test so you can learn what makes them tick, too. You'll be able to relate to them better and build closer relationships.

If you want to learn more about the Myers-Briggs Personality Inventory, there are four best-selling books that have stood the test of time. These classics are still going strong after 25+ years. All are easy to read, contain many examples, and routinely get excellent reviews.

- *Life Types* by L.K. Hirsh and J.M. Kummerow, Grand Central Publishing, 1989, 304 pages.
- *Gifts Differing* by Isabel Myers, CPP Publishers, 1980, 248 pages.
- *Type Talk* by Otto Kroeger, Dell, 1989, 304 pages.
- *Please Understand Me* by David Kiersey and Marilyn Bates, Prometheus Nemesis Publishing, 1978, 210 pages.

CPSIA information can be obtained
at www.ICGtesting.com
Printed in the USA
LVHW081835090922
728008LV00006B/841

9 780997 374520